Baby Zoo Animals

by RONNE PELTZMAN RANDALL
illustrated by DAWN HOLMES

LADYBIRD BOOKS, INC., Auburn, Maine 04210 U.S.A.
© LADYBIRD BOOKS LTD MCMLXXXVII Loughborough, Leicestershire, England

Printed in U.S.A.

Baby elephant gives her brother
a nice cool shower.

One baby giraffe reaches down
for some grass to eat.
Another reaches up
for some tasty green leaves.

The baby chimpanzees
like to climb high.

The baby zebras
have been taking a rest.
Now they're ready for a romp.

Baby kangaroo stays safe and snug in his mother's pouch.

The frisky baby tigers
roll and wrestle and play...

...but the lion cubs
are feeling lazy today.

Baby panda and her mother
love to eat bamboo leaves.

After a swim,
the baby seals like to stretch out
on the sunny rocks.

The polar bear cubs stay cool
in their icy pool.

The baby hippos have fun
wading with their mother.

Baby camel has
long, long legs.